FINISHING LINE PRESS

www.finishinglinepress.com

Dust to Dust

poems by

Bridget Dolan

Finishing Line Press
Georgetown, Kentucky

Dust to Dust

ACKNOWLEDGMENTS

Special thanks to my Granny for making this possible.

Publisher: Leah Maines

Editor: Christen Kincaid

Cover Art: Deirdre Dolan

Author Photo: Thomas Dolan

Cover Design: Elizabeth Maines McCleavy

Order online: www.finishinglinepress.com
also available on amazon.com

Author inquiries and mail orders:
Finishing Line Press
P. O. Box 1626
Georgetown, Kentucky 40324
U. S. A.

Table of Contents

Part I: Earth to Earth

Part II: Ashes to Ashes

Part I: Earth to Earth

Between the roots of my tomato plants

the worms
in my garden
do not worry
about their right
      to their body.
they are free
to exist,
eating,
sleeping,
breathing,
      as God
      intended.

Red

Mom usually forgets
that after the last frost,
we plant the tomato seeds.

so instead, in April or May,
she brings home fresh planters—
cherry, grape, heirloom tomatoes.

we move them, in June,
to the garden under the window,
in view of the laundry room.

in linen shorts and old tank tops,
we kneel in the garden, the soil cool
on our skin as we rehome the tomatoes.

I don't like to wear gloves
in the summer because I sweat,
and I lose the sensation of earth.

I bury my face in the bed, breathing
in the pollen I forget I'm allergic to
for the exsanguination of my insanity.

The Field

There's a cornfield
across the street,
across two white lines
and a yellow double,
across the street
from my parents' house.
Cars, they fly down there,
blasting stereos, taking
blind hills and turns
like they don't care
if something here dies.

So we look both ways—
                        look again,
and run faster than we ever
did on the track in gym class.
We got t-shirts, pulled up,
bulging, like aprons, full
            of split tomatoes,
and one of us has a wiffle bat,
borrowed from the garage,
and for the afternoon,
we'll pretend that we're
just like Cal Ripken, hitting
                        out of the field.

I envy you

oh, to be an earthworm
among the soil,
the twigs,
the rotting leaves,
and the maze of roots
that are home.

thou shalt not want
as an earthworm
for a Maserati.
earthworms have
no need
for combustion engines.

it is enough—
as an earthworm—
to do nothing more
than just   be.

Oh Deer

the deer who bite
the flowers
from my tomatoes
do not know
the blood I've lost
in that soil.
they do not know
how I knelt,
in the hot sun,
       for hours,
fingers in the dirt,
bare-handed,
building a home
for these seedlings.

these heirloom tomatoes,
still green this month,
are my children.
so, please, deer,
in your white-tailed
free majesty,
       leave them be.

Clovers

in the tufted,
uneven, almost
overgrowth I call
my lawn—
I crouch down,
staining my jeans
      and hunt.

clumsy fingers
fumble
through patches
of clovers,
three leaf,
three leaf,
three leaf—
      never four.

for four hours,
I looked for
those four-
armed charms,
but all I got
was an outbreak
of hives on my
      forearms.

mother earth
has no luck
for a woman
      like me.

With fuzzy feet

bees dock
on the roses
in my mother's
garden,
wetting their
delicate feet
with the love
between flowers.

shuffling, wiggling,
until their knees
turn yellow,
and they take off,
carrying
           love
to the next.

Duchesses of my garden

ladybugs, coccinellidae,
the unsung heroes
of my garden.
when those aphids—
tiny, green, angry—
come for my leaves,
you open your maw
and devour those
      demons.
you let my tomatoes,
snap peas, zucchinis,
green beans, parsnips,
and wispy carrots
         live.

Dandelion

I am the dandelion
crouching amongst the grass,
           hiding
from those thunderous blades
and the man who pushes
the lawnmower, back and forth,
in his best efforts to behead
           me.
A lucky dandelion
does not grow tall before
           she blooms,
catching eyes but out of reach,
her golden head swaying
until she becomes a memory,
useful only for that same man
           to make a wish
and make her disappear.

Sunflower

Celebrate the tall woman,
her head held high,
towering above the men
and making herself seen.

See her dance in the wind,
swaying with her strong spine,
stealing the show
       no, commanding,
       demanding
that we revere her, the queen
of the garden, the watcher,
protector, lover,
            sunflower.

Rose

we do not question
why the rose bush
has thorns, so why
do we doubt women
who have hardened
                    themselves
as protection from
this world, so cruel,
so harsh, so destructive?

beautiful buds, slowly
unfurling, understanding
what it means to bloom
on this earth—
it means plucking,
pruning, shaving away
                    her safety.
 but what is more
            captivating
than the wild rose,
in her briar, her home,
in her earthly glamor?

stop, please,
give me back
        my thorns.

Matriarch of Asteraceae

Chrysanthemums are the mothers of gardens,
the perennial presence, both delicate and fierce,
beautiful in their infinite varieties—constant.
These women are so powerful, versatile,
herbs that sprouted and shouted,
                              listen to me, child
and with each spring, as the buds slowly
appear, first one and then one thousand,
and we fall to our knees before them,
transfixed by these women, these flowers,
letting our eyes fall upon them, laid bare,
opening up, satiating cravings, curiosity,
                              Mums.

Mushroom

Toadstools,
the beckoning border
of forests' fairy rings,
fleshy, fruity,
unapologetically
     fungus.

You paint yourself
   to survive,
and yet children
come along, greedy,
beheading you and
   your family.

Red means *don't touch,*
don't put me in your
      mouth
Red means *warning,*
death is coming,
   it is too late.

Friends

In the shadow
of the overhang,
by the back corner
of the garage, there's
a colony of little
heads, poking above
the grass that the
red rumbling mower
   can't cut.
They stand tall,
in their pageboy caps,
waving hello
from their rooted
   homes.

Caress the tops
of their heads—
   don't yank,
just feel how soft
life can be when
   undisturbed.

Bogged

puddles
seem bottomless from
my home in this bog,
tucked in, like a child
ready for bed, among
peat, moss, decaying,
where the sound has
                    stopped.
in here, I am at peace,
at rest, beginning and
ending, all with the earth,
        my mother—
there is no birth, there
is no death, there is
screaming silence
and a promise
        of an eternity.

Wetlands

mires, wetlands,
bogs are
       acidic;
fens are
       alkaline,
and I took chemistry,
but Lord knows
I don't remember
much of the pH scale—
bogs, home to peat,
       pH below 7;
fens, grassy marshes,
       pH above 7;
for all that means,
ecologically, logically,
when I close my
       eyes
they are the exact
       fucking
           same.

Cemeteries

Wetlands, amongst the world's most economically valuable ecosystems and essential regulators of the global climate, are disappearing three times faster than forests.

these salt marshes,
these sea grass beds,
these arching roots
      of mangroves,
are dying.

men in c
overalls,
draining away the life,
making room for
brick townhomes—
mausoleums for
      the Earth.

pyramids of silt,
with their grey roofs,
stand austerely over
what was once
      alive.
now, urban memorials
to a man-made death—
men who insist
climate change is a hoax

Swamp

Spanish moss
blankets this
       home,
where tree roots
arch and bend,
nature's
       neighborhood
alongside the river,
brackish, fresh.

crayfish that children,
catch in rivers, bare-handed,
to show their mothers.
alligators, hungry and
       curious.
mosquitos, thirsting,
and birds that scream.

Aquifer

Every well
     runs dry
when every person
from the village
dips in their buckets
     again
           and again,
pulling out more,
more water, more life,
more from me.
and then, when they
hit dry ground, wooden
pails clanking against
parched stone,
they leave. they find
another well, and forget
how they
     killed me.

Dirt

Dirty, unclean, foul—
but how could the earth,
mother nature herself,
be anything but
                    vibrant?
Decay is just another
part of growing, and
the decomposition of
dead cells brings new
greenery, new seedlings,
new organisms, new
                    life.
When we die, when we
return to our mother,
six feet underneath,
wrapped in her embrace,
we take new first steps
towards heralding
        the new soil,
        the new future.

Planting

Tear the package open
with your teeth, girl
because you're not gonna
get a grip when your fingers
are more soil than flesh.

Bite it, get a grip
but be careful
because you better
not spill those seeds
all over. they need
to grow in the homes
we poked for them,
one index-finger-deep.

Shake a few out,
on your palm, count them
count out, one, two, three—
three seeds per home
because God can't promise
that they'll all sprout,
so you get your Plan B
and wait for the first
rainfall, wait for it,
wait for it, wait for it—
                    germinate.

But we planted in March

April showers
bring May flowers
But we planted in March,
when the frost has stopped,
but Mother Nature
still flirts with winter,
teasing, twisting, gusting—
promising rain, but maybe,
just maybe, it might snow
according to the weatherman.

But we planted in March,
on one of those odd days
where it gets up to
      75 degrees,
and we rolled up our jeans,
kicked off our socks,
yanked sweaters over
      our ears,
and kneeled in the dirt.

But we planted in March,
and maybe next week
it'll get up to 50,
so now we kneel
      in pews,
praying for sunshine,
a warm spring shower,
and seeds strong enough
to break through the cold
      and their shells.

April

April is coming, she's knocking
at the door, bellowing, demanding
we welcome her torrents
with open arms, but we close
our doors instead.

So she takes her deep breath,
righteous, rapturous,
and exhales green clouds
that scream *Run.*

Clouds that make your mother
lock the back door,
draw your curtains,
and holler for you
to haul ass downstairs.

Hurry up, goddammit,
there's a tornado coming.

April Storms

Moderate to severe thunderstorms
the weatherman says, waving
somewhat near your county,
where the city name isn't
listed on the map on TV.

A slight chance of a tornado
watch this morning
he says, conversationally,
as if the T.J. Maxx
the next town over
didn't lose its entire
                    roof.

The National Weather Service
has issued a tornado warning
for Frederick County
the television screams,
or was that your mother—
it doesn't matter, grab
your phone and blanket
and get in the bathtub
in the basement, now.

There's a funnel cloud
out the window, out a ways,
and Mom says to hurry up
and get down there and put
the Weather Channel on
                    and listen.

Listen to the earthworm, girl

When you are a child you will say that I eat dirt from my anus,

but the truth is, I'm eating what you don't want to think about—

those dead leaves that you half-assed sweeping when your mother told you,

Get a rake and get rid of all those leaves. Your father can't mow like this.

But I'm also eating the berries, fallen from the bush in the corner of your yard,

the blueberry one that the deer love to pick at, leaving half-eaten, rotting bits

to find a home in the soil, where then they become my feast.

I'm opening wide to take in the algae that you dumped in your compost pile, right

after you finished skimming the pond, except not all of it landed on the top,

some of it slid off and fell to the earth, giving me a tasty treat in this dry,

dry summer. I miss April, when the rain erupted from the sky, flooding the gardens

and giving me a ride to the sidewalk, where I could dance among the drops.

And the little boy next door, the one you tell your sister is cute, even if you don't

think so—he says to you after the spring shower that I'm like a chocolate bar,

that if you cut me in two, you'll have two of me, but that's not really true,

all you're going to do is split my digestive system, split my body, split my body

from my head. Your puppy didn't grow a second puppy when you docked its tail,

so why do you think that I would? You don't think I have a brain at all, don't you?

What is a little life, so small, so soft, so fragile, born to a garden?

Part II: Ashes to Ashes

Rest

I want to live
under the moss,
      the stones,
      the soil.
bury me
in the earth,
to breathe
and decompose,
for I am exhausted.

the whetstone
of womanhood
has ground my fingers
           to the bone.
so please,
please
please
      let me rest.

Grey

When I got older, I swear
the skies started getting
        greyer,
or maybe it was
just my eyes
glassing over the beauty
that I breathed in.

The year before last,
I tried to tell myself
that a cactus
in a dorm room
        was enough.

That if I filled
this empty apartment
with enough green,
it would be like
I was kneeling in dirt
with my mother
        except
she was drinking,
and I was drinking,
and I couldn't remember
how warm cold soil
was when your fingers
        had gone numb.

Cry, baby

in a summer shower,
I stand
          barefoot
on the fragmented
stone of my patio,
remove my glasses,
and lift my face
          to the sky.
I soak in the tears
that the Earth cries
for me, for us—
tears for children
that forget to say
how much we love
our green mother.

I let her wash me,
cleanse my soul
and set me free
from my sins,
my doubt, the guilt
I carry like a too-heavy
          backpack.
she caresses me,
raindrops sliding down
the slope of my nose,
and she reminds me
that it is okay for me
to cry along with her,
to shake off the anguish
          of existence
          and be reborn.

A droopy little cactus, with fuzzy feelers

You're standing in line at the Home Depot again, and you're cradling the saddest succulent on the shelf because maybe fixing it will make you feel better about how you can't seem to fix yourself. 'Cause honey, that bottle of gin doesn't love you no matter how much you kiss it, and you can only pour so much through a gaping hole before you realize that it isn't filling anything. So you go out and buy another fucking plant because it's only 11 a.m., and, you know, it's not alcoholism if you only drink after noon—that's just what everyone else does, right? And you're in line at Home Depot, blasted by orange, praying that the cashier doesn't recognize you, and besides, you went to Lowe's last week so it's not like you have an addiction. And the night before last, you had the cheapest bottle of wine you could find, one of those dark red mixes that tastes like a crow dying in your mouth, you're mixing it up. And you're not drinking alone—you got every windowsill in your home filled with plants, and they're not going to tell you that you're not making the party fun anymore, that you're getting drunk too quickly, that everyone else is there to just have a good time so why can't you? And now you're up to bat at the register, and this cashier's expression is dead, but the one at the register two over gives you a sad look that you pretend not to see. And you dig out your wallet, hunting for your credit card, because last night's gin was poured straight from the dredges of your paycheck, and what's a little more debt, anyways? Insert the chip, already. Damn your shaky hands.

Again

I must've broken the first pot
I picked up when I picked up
        gardening again.
Terracotta, the cheap kind,
because broken brains
need baby-proofing.
I switched to plastic then—
it cracks, but it's even
cheaper, and when you're
so desperate, you need cheap.

I bought soil, stared at the shelf
for so damn long, at the products
                the price tags
as if I wasn't going to buy
the cheapest one anyways,
and so I nestle it against my hip,
like a baby I'll never carry,
and bring my newborn home.

I stood at my trunk, in a parking
lot, praying no one could see,
and then I dug my hands deep
into the dirt, dry and wanting.
I took fistfuls of it, making a bed
for new life, for my new life,
because I wanted to try, so badly,
and I need something new
        to stop my thinking.

Watering

There's this beauty
in watering plants
that I never thought
much about before
I stopped watering
    myself.

Acid rain was bringing
those grey clouds,
but then, I dumped
the rain down the
   toilet,
and bought a new
glass bottle—water,
something I could share
something I could imbibe
without drinking alone
or inviting bad weather.

I'm not ready
for a watering can,
   not yet,
because I still can't
do this alone, can't
live in this desert
   all by myself.

A $9.98 cactus ensemble from Home Depot

I wake up every morning
and stare down into
that little orange bottle
filled with little green pills
and I think to myself,
I could take all of these
and then maybe I wouldn't
feel so damn thirsty
all   the   time

and stare at the wall,
cream paint, chipping,
and stare out the window,
sunny, birds singing,
succulents
          on the sill.

A life that needs me,
more than I need it,
so maybe that bottle
can wait until tomorrow.

Clay

If you were
to reach down
and stick your hand
into my chest, all
you would find
is clay,
like when you
dig too deep
in the garden,
and the soil

           stops.

It's dirt, yes,
some life,
but it's not going
to grow new life,
not the kind
you want.
All those insects
you pretend
don't exist
until they brush up
against your now-bony
fingers
when you're digging
out rocks
from that
long-forgotten
garden under
the laundry room
        window.

Pre-dawn ponderings

in the early morning,
when the soil is still cool,
damp with dew from the
            witching hour,
you will find me,
elbow-deep, whispering
to my snap peas, these
sweet green therapists,
and maybe not the best
active listeners, but
the ones who lend an ear
are often those without.

and so, still in pajamas,
on my knees,
in a holey cotton
Myrtle Beach
tank top and
now dirt-smudged
Superman shorts,
I confide, whisper
about my nightmare
where the earth stopped
and time ripped me
from my bones—
making me a woman
            without a home.

The Wailing Woman

I do not know why
the willow weeps,
but I hear her
on nights I don't sleep,
when the moon fails
          to rise
and my breaths
match hers.

In a silent house, I ache
to wail along with her,
to exhale the tragedy
of our existence.
Instead, my jaw
is wired shut
by souls asleep.

In the mornings,
I stand under her,
socks soaked by
midnight dew—
          her tears—
and rest my palm
against her trunk,
saying, *I hear you.*

Look

I stopped looking
in corners, under logs,
in the slinking shadows,
for those patches of life,
of mushrooms, of weeds,
of things I thought best left
        forgotten.

As you get older,
they tell you *stop looking*
at your feet all the time,
the world is up above
but what isn't said
is that there is a whole
world, brimming
with life, right underneath
        your feet.

Dig

Dig your fingers in,
       both hands,
plunge them deep
into the soil, feeling
the change in the earth.
Feel the shift of warmth,
       a sun-soaked blanket,
to a cold, hardened, damp
bed of darkened life,
life that still exists,
       flourishes,
even when you can't see
its work until the first
sprouts break through
that light cover.

Earthworms, grubs, and
so much more, teeming
underneath your feet,
underneath your fingers,
muscling through the clay
that stops your own hands.
       Living.

Rain

when the rain
                    falls
I go outside,
no umbrella,
and face the sky.
I step into
my garden
           barefoot,
with my toes,
wriggling,
in the wet soil,
feeling the life
in my
           sole.

Feel

Raindrops on the back
of my neck bring
tears—each one,
a distinct, discrete
          sensation.
Cold, a pinprick of
weight, something
                    real.

The wind, blowing
through the mess
of overgrowth that
lines the base of my
neck, begging for
a buzz, twirling.
          a chill
                    hair raised.

Hands-on

I dig my fingers in,
accumulating soil—
      dark brown,
        nitrogen-rich,
under my fingernails,
covering my knuckles,
my own DIY gardening
      gloves.
with rubber, maybe leather,
over your hands, you can't
feel the earth burrow
into the grooves in your
      fingerprints,
marking you as her own.
you cannot feel the softness
of an earthworm dancing
      on your palm,
nor the dampness of life
reborn, remade in this
small patch underneath
      my window.

Macroscopic Microcosm

aphids,
grubs,
earthworms
all have no need
      for your guns.

life in a garden
does not want
      for firearms
no Ak-47, no M16,
not even
a revolver.

there is no six-shot,
no ammo, no
children running
for their lives.

because first,
there was   Columbine

and then,
there was   Sandy Hook

not long
after   Marjory
      Stoneman
      Douglas.

tell me,
what child
needs a gun more
than an earthworm?

Bottoms Up

I swallow twenty-five milligrams
      of crabgrass
every morning to get myself out
      of bed.
I wash it down along with a drop
      of bottled sunlight
to ignite photosynthesis in the pit
      of my stomach.
At night, a round white pill
      of fertilizer
tucks into the soil, keeping the
      pH steady,
keeping the dopamine in check—
      no flooding.

Coming Home

my home is tucked away,
hiding between hills,
blanketed by corn.

the side of the house
is lined with a woodpile
that turns to growth,

raspberries and wild
strawberries that creep
through a brambled mess,

screaming *I'm here*
I am still surviving,
returning each summer.

garter snakes slither
behind stacked logs,
prowling for field mice

that dare to break into
the house and hoard
dog food in the walls.

there is little grey here—
all browns and greens,
sometimes reds and blues.

this is not a place for loud
cars or trains or even airplanes.
sometimes, hot air balloons.

that does not mean that quiet
is the prevalent sound—only
that you need to listen to hear.

Garden Hose

The garden hose is green,
formerly coiled, now kinked,
winding through the grass
like the world's weirdest snake.

She stretches, across the jagged
patio, between the white legs of
the outdoor furniture, over the
sentimental stepping stone.

I stand, at the edge of the garden,
barefoot, my toes wiggling in the lawn,
reveling in the way the grass dances
in between them, tickling me.

The head is in my right hand, my
left reaches to hold the body,
keeping her steady as she lurches
and thrashes—the water's on now.

I squeeze the nozzle, fighting the rust
that would much rather not be moved.
I spray the zucchini a little rougher,
the small carrot sprouts gentler.

And when each plant, from the tomatoes
to the green beans, even the snap peas,
are watered, I turn the hose downward,
to my toes, and make mud just to feel
                    the earth.

Lot 7003

the steps of the back patio
                    are crooked.
they are attached to the foundation
of the house, and so they shift
with the earth, with floods that
rebuild the land our house
                  is built on.
land, it is land, what it was is
the putting green of an old golf
course, and it still has the hole
for scoring — only now it lives
right next to the odd, evergreen
bush I brought home in the third
grade, not even knowing what
this sapling wrapped in a damp
paper towel might one day
                turn out to be.
but this tiny, almost wilting
seedling grew hardier and stronger,
and I knew, I knew that I would too
and then
                        I did.

Bullfrogs

dusk, when the sky
paints itself
      pink,
is the bullfrogs'
favorite time
to put on a
performance.
with the setting
      of the sun,
they start
their solemn song,
standing on
their fractured
      stone stage
that rims the pond
just past
the patio's   edge.

I sit on the steps,
empty palm
      yearning
for a beer, instead
holding a sweet tea,
and I listen
because I know
how they want,
how they need,
how they
      beg.
I look at my mother's
ashtray, balanced on
the step, overflowing
with half-smoked
sticks, and I imagine
dying   just for a minute.

The Willow

The willow stands
     hunched,
     cowed
like a woman
boxed in by boys
playing at being men,
building a hedge
of misogynistic guilt,
       cowing cowardice
designed to break
off her branches
and dig up her roots.
She is stripped
     of her leaves,
     her dignity,
her right   to exist.

How dare a willow
stand so tall,
     so strong,
so unafraid to weather
the storms of a changing
     climate
where we carve letters
into the bodies of women
     decided unworthy of
     carrying our mantle.
Yet we do not think
about the "A" that
we award ourselves,
that "A" that brands
us   woman
lesser   never enough.

Are we not all   the willow?

Callous

Even when it rains, I only ever go out onto the back patio in my bare feet, ignoring my mother's call of *Put on shoes before you go outside* that I've been hearing since I was five — I'm not going to put on shoes, not even dad's too-big navy blue crocs that live by the back sliding door. *I'm building calluses to protect my feet,* I say, even though there's no one to listen anymore, no one wondering why I think I need calluses when all the work I've been doing is sitting behind a desk or at the kitchen table or in bed, technically still at a desk even if it's just my beaten wooden lap desk. But there aren't desks outside, there aren't desks out where it rains, and it's a liberation that I'm not letting go of. I need those calluses, I need my square, too-wide-for-most-shoes feet to be stronger because I need them to carry me and I don't know where I'm going, but I'll be damned if I don't go.

Changes

I was seventeen when
        I lost my mind.

I was nineteen when
        I met the doctor.

I was twenty-one when
        I learned that

I will never get it back
        and that's okay.

I was twenty-one when
        I picked up a trowel.

I scooped out the cheapest soil
        into a plastic planter.

I was twenty-one when
        I killed cacti.

I underwatered them, turns out
        you can do that.

I was twenty-three when
        I stopped trying so hard.

I decided to let myself live
        and stick my hands in the dirt.

earth

I came from the earth,
       so did you.
We live on the Earth,
capital-E Earth, but
when we stand in
the grass and wiggle
our toes, we are
in the *earth*, home,
               mother.

Yes, Earth is the
planet, the globe,
our rock hurtling
around the sun,
       365.24 days,
but the *earth* is
the life beneath
our soles, what
we feel with our
palms when we reach
out for   another.

earth—
dirt, dust,
mud, sand,
silt, soil,
       the *earth*
is our birthplace
and   the *earth*
is our resting place.

Notes:

The epigraph of "Cemeteries" is from the United Nations report on the disappearance of wetlands.

Acknowledgements:

To my parents, Mary and Paul Dolan, thank you so much for your constant support through my ups and downs, many as they have been and will be.

To my sister, Dee Dee Dolan, thank you for a beautiful photo for my cover and constantly hyping up my poetry.

To my brother, Tommy Dolan, thank you for humoring my need for an entire photoshoot with the dog.

To my older sister, Maddy Dolan, thank you for keeping me humble and grounded by reminding me that I am not, in fact, the god of poetry. You have kept me from getting a big head all our lives.

To Morgan Russell, thank you for reading every poem I've ever sent you and constantly sharing your love for them and me. You sat by me, quite literally, as I edited this collection, and I would not have made it here without your support.

To my poetry professors, Dr. JoAnn Balingit and Claire McCabe, thank you for helping me grow my art and blossom into the poet I am. I would not have discovered my own style or found the confidence to experiment without your help.

Bridget Dolan is a poet and mental health worker from New Market, Maryland. She has degrees in English and astronomy from the University of Delaware. Bridget started writing poetry at a young age in elementary school, but it wasn't until late in her college career when she started studying it and began her devotion to it. Her work appears in the University of Delaware's literary journals *Caesura* and *The Main Street Journal* as well as the online literary magazine *Marías at Sampaguitas*. She takes her inspiration from her family and her childhood home and dug deep into her roots to bring Dust to Dust to fruition. She grew up gardening, and despite killing cacti, kept on trying—her green thumb is closer to brown, but she's still trying. She currently lives at home with her family and two dogs, Maggie and Moose. *Dust to Dust* is her first collection.

www.ingramcontent.com/pod-product-compliance
Lightning Source LLC
Chambersburg PA
CBHW021203090426
42740CB00008B/1206